JOSEPH CASTLE

Joseph Castle is one of the country's finest arrangers for the classical guitar. The arrangements contained in this text reflect both his comprehensive knowledge of the guitar and of music in general. We know of no other book that blends the guitar into its rightful place in the development of western music. We are indebted to Mr. Castle for the hours of research undertaken and for his excellence in adapting symphonic and piano scores to the guitar fingerboard.

Mel Bay

Copyright 1971
Mel Bay Publications, Inc.
International Copyright Secured - All Rights Reserved
Printed in U.S.A.

2

Contents

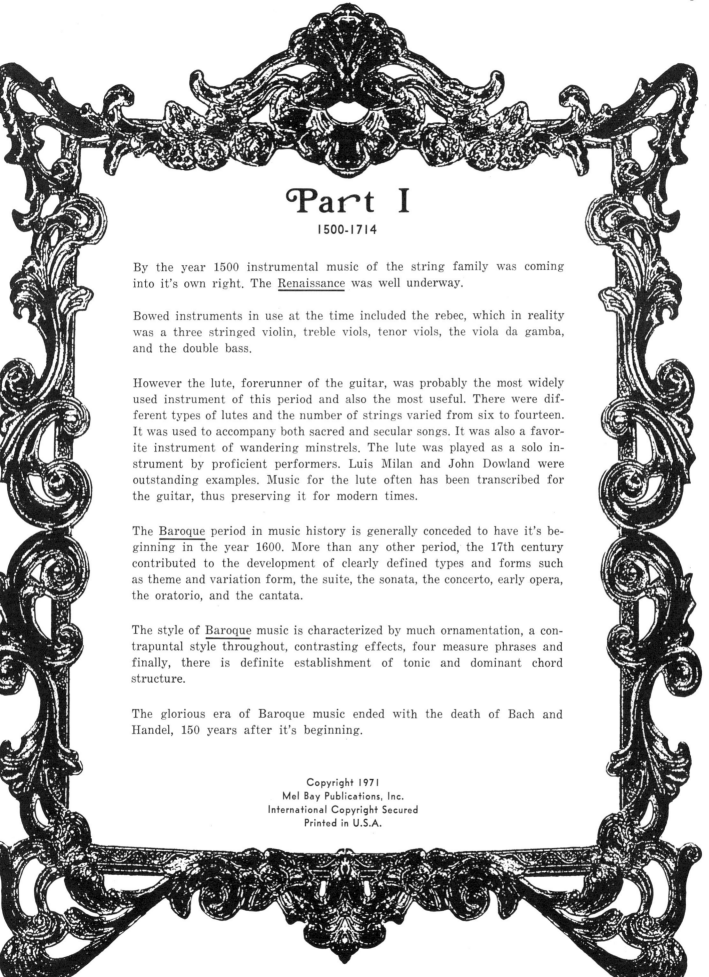

Part I
1500-1714

By the year 1500 instrumental music of the string family was coming into it's own right. The Renaissance was well underway.

Bowed instruments in use at the time included the rebec, which in reality was a three stringed violin, treble viols, tenor viols, the viola da gamba, and the double bass.

However the lute, forerunner of the guitar, was probably the most widely used instrument of this period and also the most useful. There were different types of lutes and the number of strings varied from six to fourteen. It was used to accompany both sacred and secular songs. It was also a favorite instrument of wandering minstrels. The lute was played as a solo instrument by proficient performers. Luis Milan and John Dowland were outstanding examples. Music for the lute often has been transcribed for the guitar, thus preserving it for modern times.

The Baroque period in music history is generally conceded to have it's beginning in the year 1600. More than any other period, the 17th century contributed to the development of clearly defined types and forms such as theme and variation form, the suite, the sonata, the concerto, early opera, the oratorio, and the cantata.

The style of Baroque music is characterized by much ornamentation, a contrapuntal style throughout, contrasting effects, four measure phrases and finally, there is definite establishment of tonic and dominant chord structure.

The glorious era of Baroque music ended with the death of Bach and Handel, 150 years after it's beginning.

PAVANA

LUIS MILAN
(1500- 1561)

LARGO

from " STABAT MATER "

PALESTRINA
(1515 - 1594)

THE EARLE OF SALISBURY

WILLIAM BYRDE
(1558 - 1623)

GAGLIARDA

FRESCOBALDI
(1583 - 1644)

SUITE NO. II

ESAIAS REUSNER
(1636 – 1679)

ALLEMANDA

COURANDA

SARABANDA

GIGUE

SARABANDE

ROBERT DE VISÉE
(1650 - 1725)

LE PETIT RIEN

FRANCOIS COUPERIN
(1668 - 1733)

Allegretto

CARNIVAL

FRANCOIS COUPERIN
(1668 - 1733)

Tune 6th String
down to D

Allegro

RONDINO

JEAN PHILIPPE RAMEAU
(1683 - 1764)

BOURRÉE

J. S. BACH
(1685 - 1750)

TWO-PART INVENTIONS

J. S. BACH

PRELUDE AND FUGUE

J. S. BACH

Prelude

FUGUE

LARGO

(" Xerxes ")

G. F. HÄNDEL
(1685 - 1759)

SUITE FOR THE LUTE
OVERTURE

PHILIPP DE RICHÉE
(1695 - ?)

Largo

Allegro

SARABANDE

20

BOURRÉE

GAVOTTE

MINUET AND RONDO

D. C. al Fine

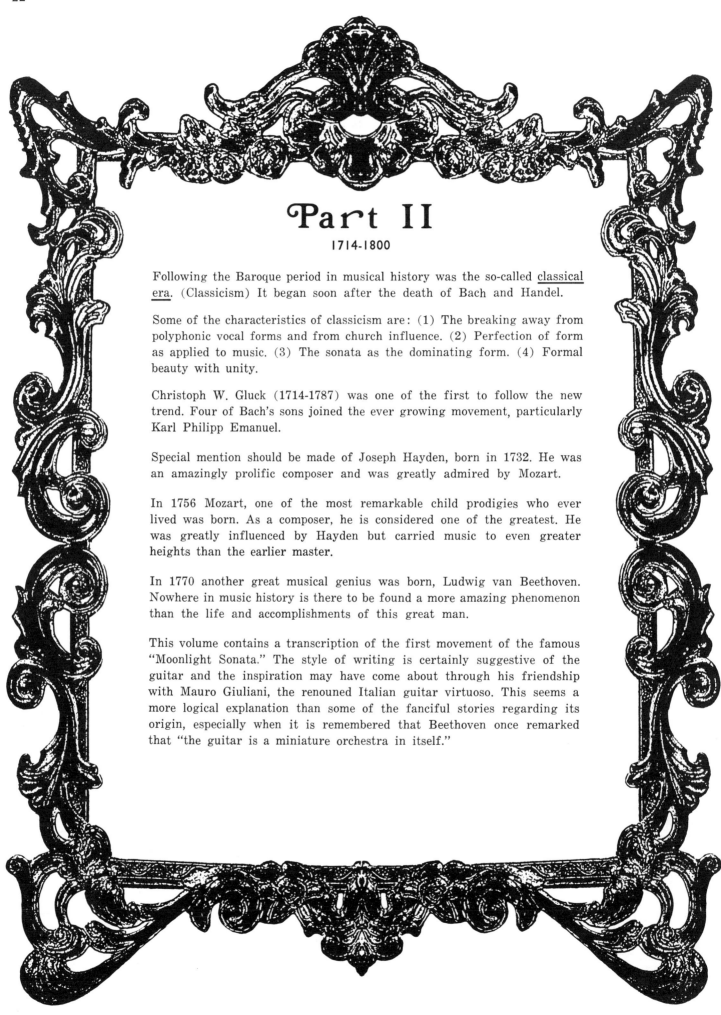

Part II
1714-1800

Following the Baroque period in musical history was the so-called <u>classical era</u>. (Classicism) It began soon after the death of Bach and Handel.

Some of the characteristics of classicism are: (1) The breaking away from polyphonic vocal forms and from church influence. (2) Perfection of form as applied to music. (3) The sonata as the dominating form. (4) Formal beauty with unity.

Christoph W. Gluck (1714-1787) was one of the first to follow the new trend. Four of Bach's sons joined the ever growing movement, particularly Karl Philipp Emanuel.

Special mention should be made of Joseph Hayden, born in 1732. He was an amazingly prolific composer and was greatly admired by Mozart.

In 1756 Mozart, one of the most remarkable child prodigies who ever lived was born. As a composer, he is considered one of the greatest. He was greatly influenced by Hayden but carried music to even greater heights than the earlier master.

In 1770 another great musical genius was born, Ludwig van Beethoven. Nowhere in music history is there to be found a more amazing phenomenon than the life and accomplishments of this great man.

This volume contains a transcription of the first movement of the famous "Moonlight Sonata." The style of writing is certainly suggestive of the guitar and the inspiration may have come about through his friendship with Mauro Giuliani, the renouned Italian guitar virtuoso. This seems a more logical explanation than some of the fanciful stories regarding its origin, especially when it is remembered that Beethoven once remarked that "the guitar is a miniature orchestra in itself."

DANCE OF THE BLESSED SPIRITS

CHR. W. GLUCK
(1714 - 1787)

ANDANTE

J. HAYDN
(1732–1809)

GAVOTTE

F.J.GOSSEC
(1733-1829)

AIR

W.A.MOZART
(1756 – 1791)

PRESTO

W.A.MOZART

MINUET

(ORIGINAL IN G)

L. VAN BEETHOVEN
(1770 - 1827)

Minuet D.C.

ALLEGRETTO
(FROM 7TH SYMPHONY)

L. VAN BEETHOVEN

SONATA QUASI UNA FANTASIA

(THE "MOONLIGHT" SONATA)

L. VAN BEETHOVEN
Op. 27 No. 2

Adagio Sostenuto

ANDANTE GRAZIOSO

F. CARULLI
(1770–1841)

FUGHETTO

F. CARULLI

RONDO

F. CARULLI

PRELUDE NO. 1

F. MOLINO
(1775-1847)

Allegretto

PRELUDE NO. 5

F. MOLINO

STUDY NO. VII

(OPUS 31)

F. SOR
(1778-1839)

Moderato

LARGHETTO

F. SOR

ANDANTE

F. SOR

ESTUDIO

F. SOR

ANDANTINO

FERNANDO SOR
(1778 – 1839)

ESTUDIO IN C MAJOR

F. SOR

Andante

poco rit.

ADAGIO

(FROM " GRAND SONATA ")

Opus 22

F. SOR

SONATINA

M. GIULIANI
(1780–1840)

Allegro Moderato

ALLEGRETTO

M. GIULIANI

THEME AND VARIATIONS

ANTON DIABELLI
(1781 - 1858)

SONATA

I

N. PAGANINI
(1784 - 1840)

Allegro Moderato

II

III

ROMANZA

Andante

N. PAGANINI

STUDY

D. AGUADO
(1784 - 1849)

ARPEGGIO ETUDE

D. AGUADO

MELODY TO A BELOVED

C.M. VON WEBER
(1786 - 1826)

CAPRICE NO. 1
(Opus 20)

LUIGI LEGNANI
(1790 – 1877)

CAPRICE NO. 12
(Opus 20)

LUIGI LEGNANI

Allegro non tanto

MINUET

M. CARCASSI
(1792 - 1853)

Moderato

COUNTRY DANCE

M. CARCASSI

CAPRICE IN E MINOR

(Opus 26, No. 3)

M. CARCASSI

Moderato with expression

BAGATELLE

H. MARSCHNER
(1795 - 1861)

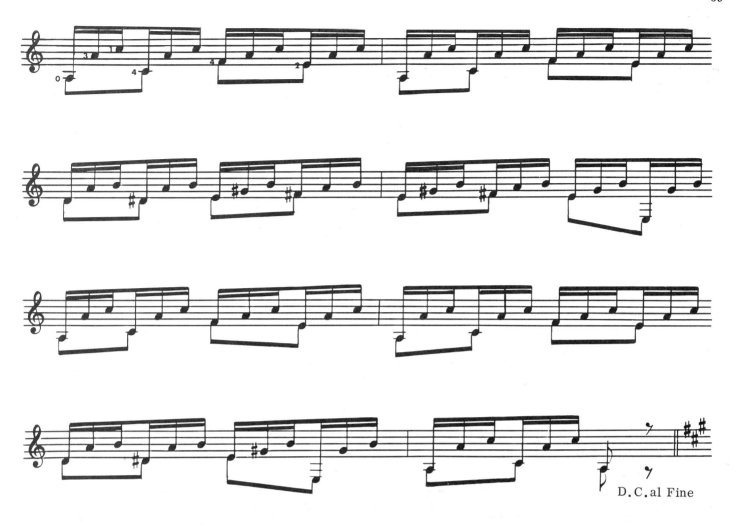

WALTZ

FRANZ SCHUBERT
(1797 – 1828)

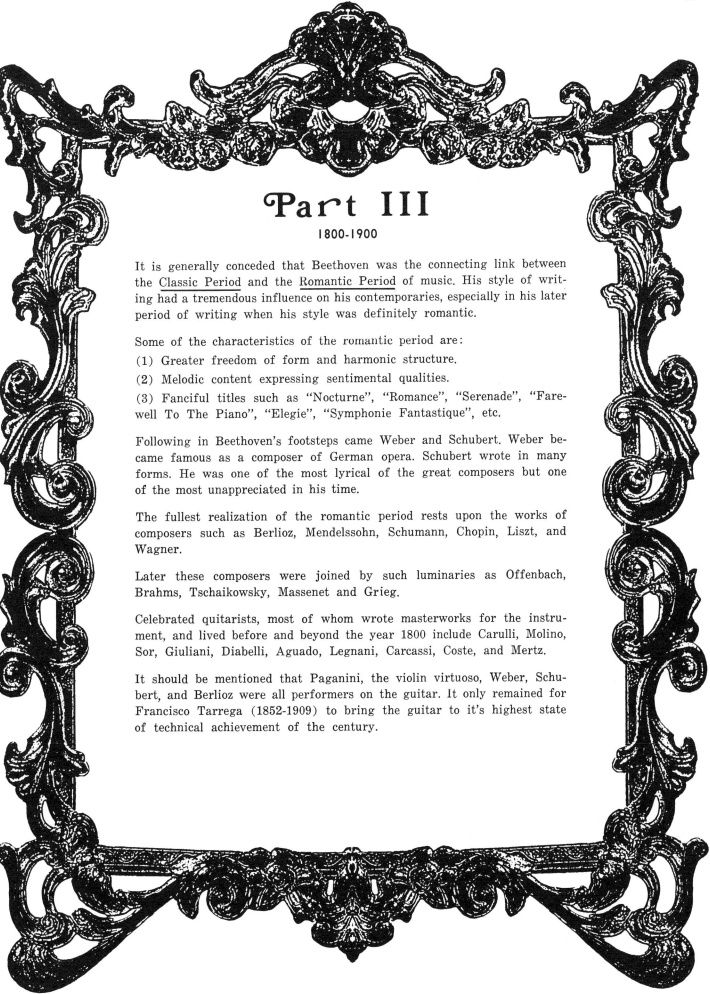

Part III

1800-1900

It is generally conceded that Beethoven was the connecting link between the Classic Period and the Romantic Period of music. His style of writing had a tremendous influence on his contemporaries, especially in his later period of writing when his style was definitely romantic.

Some of the characteristics of the romantic period are:

(1) Greater freedom of form and harmonic structure.

(2) Melodic content expressing sentimental qualities.

(3) Fanciful titles such as "Nocturne", "Romance", "Serenade", "Farewell To The Piano", "Elegie", "Symphonie Fantastique", etc.

Following in Beethoven's footsteps came Weber and Schubert. Weber became famous as a composer of German opera. Schubert wrote in many forms. He was one of the most lyrical of the great composers but one of the most unappreciated in his time.

The fullest realization of the romantic period rests upon the works of composers such as Berlioz, Mendelssohn, Schumann, Chopin, Liszt, and Wagner.

Later these composers were joined by such luminaries as Offenbach, Brahms, Tschaikowsky, Massenet and Grieg.

Celebrated quitarists, most of whom wrote masterworks for the instrument, and lived before and beyond the year 1800 include Carulli, Molino, Sor, Giuliani, Diabelli, Aguado, Legnani, Carcassi, Coste, and Mertz.

It should be mentioned that Paganini, the violin virtuoso, Weber, Schubert, and Berlioz were all performers on the guitar. It only remained for Francisco Tarrega (1852-1909) to bring the guitar to it's highest state of technical achievement of the century.

ANDANTINO

F. HORETZKY
(1800 - 1871)

PRELUDIO

Allegro

NAPOLEON COSTE
(1806 - 1883)

ROMANCE

I.K. MERTZ
(1806 - 1856)

Andante

PRELUDE NO. 4

F. CHOPIN
(1810 - 1849)

PRELUDE NO.20

(Opus 28, No.20)

F. CHOPIN

SOLDIER'S MARCH

R. SCHUMANN
(1810 – 1856)

BARCAROLE

J. OFFENBACH
(1819 – 1880)

THEME FROM 1ST SYMPHONY

J. BRAHMS
(1833-1897)

WALTZ IN A MAJOR

(Opus 39, No. 15)

J. BRAHMS

KUJAWIAK
(SECOND MAZURKA)

H. Wieniawski
(1834 - 1880)

Allegretto

THEME FROM SIXTH SYMPHONY

(PATHETIQUE)

P.I.TSCHAIKOWSKY
(1840 - 1893)

Tune 6th string
down to D

HUMORESQUE

(Opus 10, No. 2)

P. TSCHAIKOWSKY

Allegretto scherzando

D.C. al Fine

ELÉGIE

JULES MASSENET
(1842 - 1912)

HOW TO PLAY THE HARMONICS : Numbers in circles indicate string they are on. The first three are located above the 12th fret. The last three are located above the 5th fret. Use a combination of nail and rest strokes and pluck closer to the bridge than normally. The notes above the 5th fret may also be found above the imaginary 24th fret.

J. C.

ANITRA'S DANCE

(From "PEER GYNT" Suite I)

EDVARD GRIEG
(1843 - 1907)

cresc. (sequential fingering)

MARCH

XAVAR SCHARWENKA
(1850 - 1924)

Moderato

PRELUDE IN G MAJOR

F. TARREGA
(1852-1909)

SCHERZO

DAMAS-TARREGA

RECUERDOS DE LA ALHAMBRA

F. TARREGA

Andante (m.m. ♩=76-84)

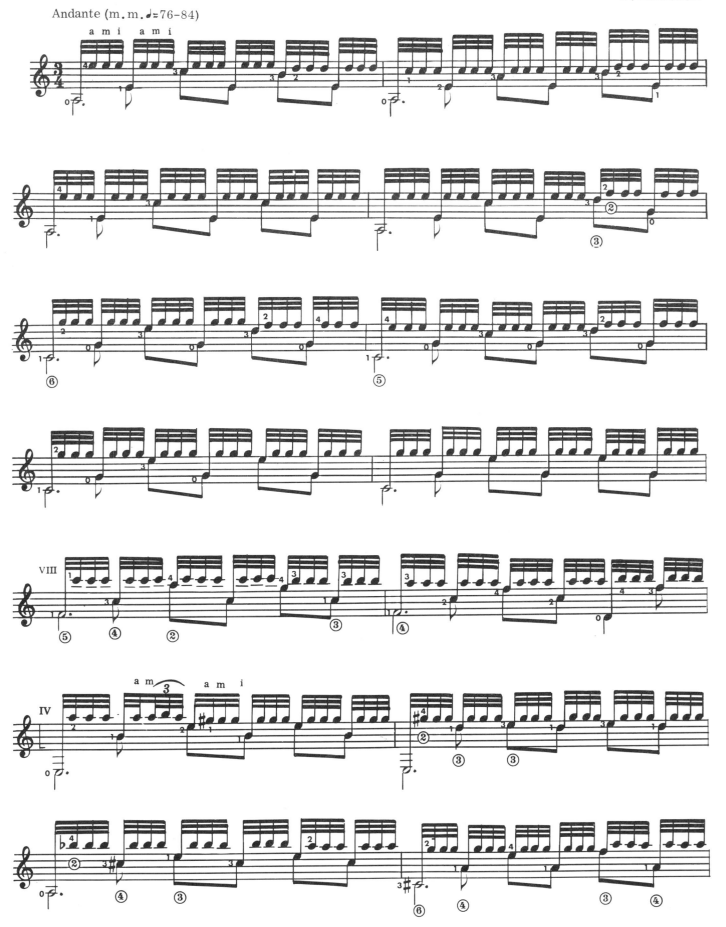

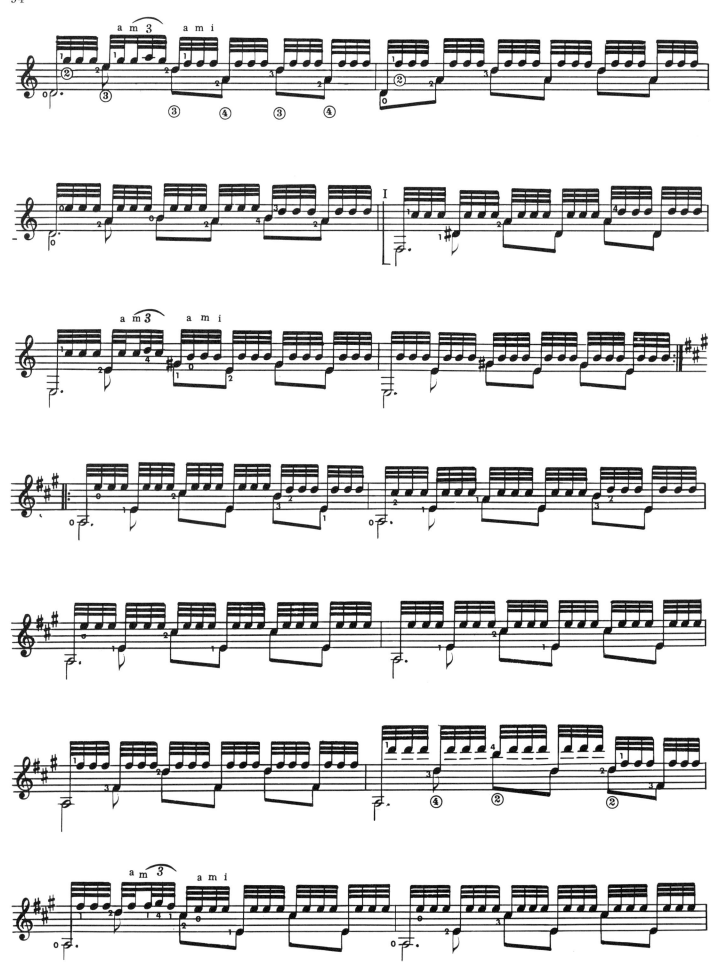

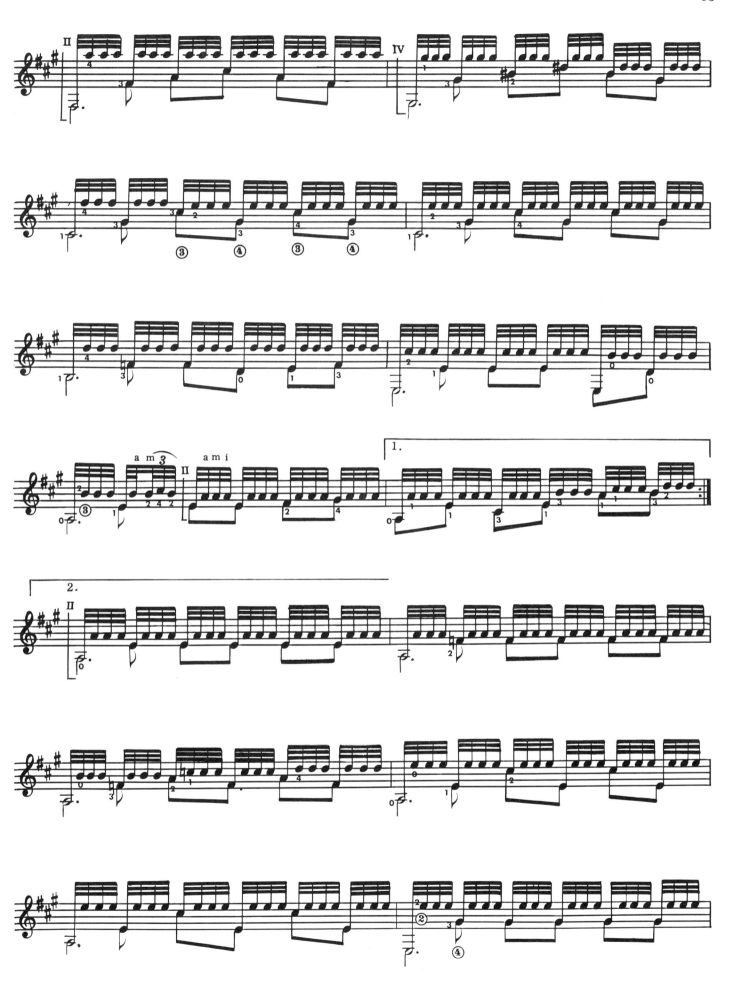

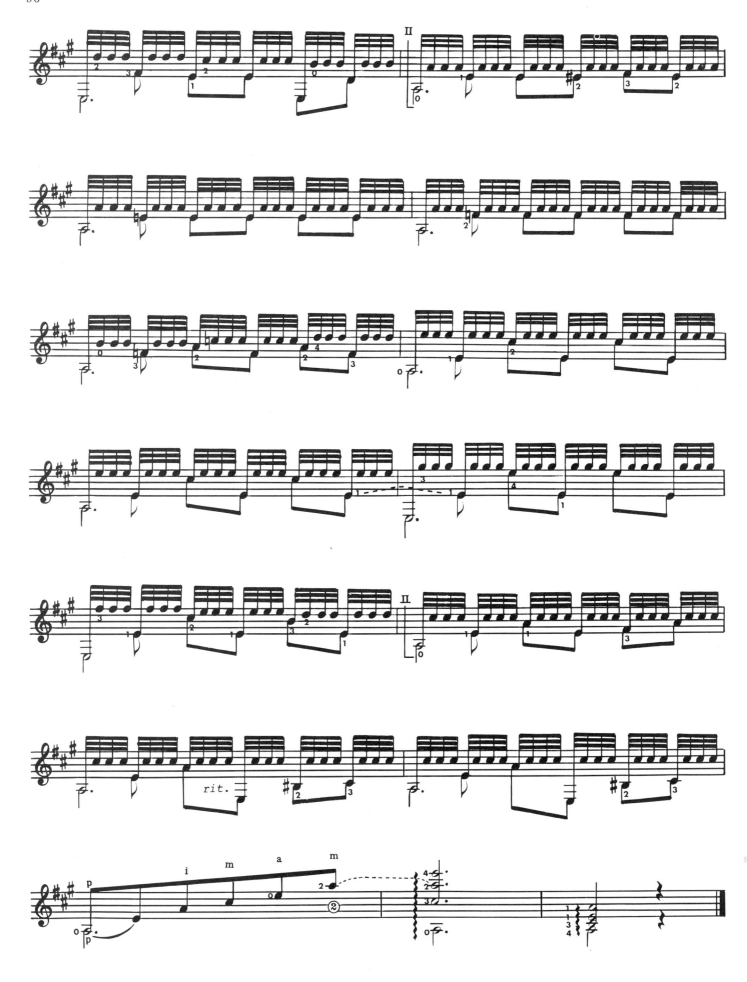